# Can I tell you about ADHD?

## Can I tell you about...?

*The "Can I tell you about...?" series offers simple introductions to a range of limiting conditions. Friendly characters invite readers to learn about their experiences of living with a particular condition and how they would like to be helped and supported. These books serve as excellent starting points for family and classroom discussions.*

*other books in the Can I tell you about...? series*

**Can I tell you about Asperger Syndrome?**
**A guide for friends and family**
*Jude Welton*
Foreword by Elizabeth Newson
Illustrated by Jane Telford
ISBN 978 1 84310 206 9
eISBN 978 1 84642 422 9

**Can I tell you about Asthma?**
**A guide for friends, family and professionals**
*Lesley Mills*
Illustrated by Rosy Salaman
ISBN 978 1 84905 350 1
eISBN 978 0 85700 744 5

**Can I tell you about Epilepsy?**
**A guide for friends, family and professionals**
*Kate Lambert*
Illustrated by Scott Hellier
ISBN 978 1 84905 309 9
eISBN 978 0 85700 648 6

**Can I tell you about Selective Mutism?**
**A guide for friends, family and professionals**
*Maggie Johnson and Alison Wintgens*
Illustrated by Robyn Gallow
ISBN 978 1 84905 289 4
eISBN 978 0 85700 611 0

# Can I tell you about ADHD?

A guide for friends, family and professionals

SUSAN YARNEY

Illustrated by Chris Martin

Jessica Kingsley *Publishers*
London and Philadelphia

First published in 2013
by Jessica Kingsley Publishers
73 Collier Street
London N1 9BE, UK
and
400 Market Street, Suite 400
Philadelphia, PA 19106, USA

*www.jkp.com*

**Library of Congress Cataloging in Publication Data**
A CIP catalog record for this book is available
from the Library of Congress

**British Library Cataloguing in Publication Data**
A CIP catalogue record for this book is
available from the British Library

ISBN 978 1 84905 359 4
eISBN 978 0 85700 708 7

Printed and bound by Bell and Bain Ltd, Glasgow

To my sons Daniel and Samuel for your never-ending patience when listening to my stories.
My parents for giving me a solid foundation.
Emre (Askim) for believing in me.
All the children/young people with ADHD/ADD we work with in East/North Hertfordshire.
Working with you teaches me new things every day – things not found in any textbook.

# Acknowledgements

Thanks to Mrs Susan McKay of Whitehall School, Cambridgeshire, for your helpful comments and contributions.

A big thank you to Mr David Entwistle for your part in this book's journey.

Thank you to all my work colleagues for your encouragement and support, especially to Dr Inyang Takon for continuing to inspire me to strive for the best for our children and young people with ADHD.

Finally, thanks to Lucy Buckroyd and all JKP staff for your help and also to Chris Martin for his lovely illustrations.

# The Story of Fidgety Philip

"Let me see if Philip can
Be a little gentleman;
Let me see if he is able
To sit still for once at table":
Thus Papa bade Phil behave;
And Mamma looked very grave.
But fidgety Phil,
He won't sit still;
He wriggles,
And giggles,
And then, I declare,
Swings backwards and forwards,
And tilts up his chair,
Just like any rocking-horse –
"Philip! I am getting cross!"
See the naughty, restless child
Growing still more rude and wild,
Till his chair falls over quite.
Philip screams with all his might,
Catches at the cloth, but then
That makes matters worse again.
Down upon the ground they fall,
Glasses, plates, knives, forks, and all.
How Mamma did fret and frown,
When she saw them tumbling down!
And Papa made such a face!
Philip is in sad disgrace.
Where is Philip, where is he?
Fairly covered up you see!
Cloth and all are lying on him;
He has pulled down all upon him.
What a terrible to-do!

Dishes, glasses, snapt in two!
Here a knife, and there a fork!
Philip, this is cruel work.
Table all so bare, and ah!
Poor Papa and poor Mamma
Look quite cross, and wonder how
They shall have their dinner now.

Heinrich Hoffman, 1845

# Contents

"Hi, my name is Ben and I have a condition with a long name called attention deficit hyperactivity disorder or ADHD for short.

Some people refer to it as attention deficit disorder or ADD, which is ADHD without the 'H' or hyperactivity."

"Before I tell you about ADHD, I want to tell you more about myself.

My name is actually Benjamin but I prefer being called Ben.

I live with my parents and my four-year-old twin sisters in a big town.

I love playing football every Saturday and I'm currently the top goal scorer in my football team.

I wish I could play football every day because I'm happiest when I'm doing things that require a lot of energy.

My hobbies are swimming, football, skateboarding and art. I like art because it helps me to express my feelings and also focus on schoolwork.

Although I have ADHD, I'm just like any other child."

"Ben aka (also known as...)

I am known by several nicknames because of my ADHD. I'm sure you've heard of a few of them."

"Having ADHD means that I sometimes behave in a certain way that makes me stand out. My family and teachers often call me 'naughty'.

Sometimes I find it very hard to control some of my behaviour and feel really sad when I upset someone and get into trouble a lot.

Having ADHD can make me feel less confident.

Teachers who do not know me say I'm a troublemaker and keep me in class during playtime. Some of my classmates upset me by saying unkind things about me.

This is why I want to tell you more about ADHD, so you can understand and help me."

"Grown-ups, especially teachers, who meet
me for the first time may think I'm being
naughty as I find it difficult to remain in
my seat or not fiddle with something."

"Sitting still in my classroom chair makes me feel really tired and causes me to lose concentration in lessons.

Fiddling with something in class can help me focus and is not meant to disrupt lessons.

Having ADHD makes it harder to do certain things such as sitting still for long periods in class and remembering not to call out during lessons when you know an answer to a question.

I am trying very hard, so please be patient.

I feel very sad when I am told I am 'naughty' or have 'challenging behaviours' and cause 'low-level disruption' in class, especially by people who do not know me very well.

My parents said when I was much younger I had very bad tantrums, especially when I didn't get my own way or have their complete attention."

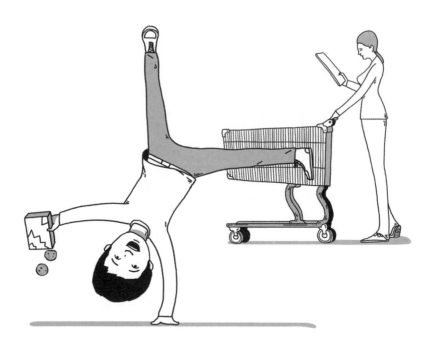

"On shopping trips, my mum's always
reminding me not to touch things. I find
it really hard to ignore all the activity and
noises in the shops. I love doing cartwheels,
particularly in shops with large floor spaces,
but this usually annoys assistants."

"'Hyper' is short for 'hyperactive', which is the letter 'H' in ADHD.

My nan calls me her 'full of beans' Benjie.

As you know, cars, lorries and aeroplanes need motor engines to help them move fast.

I can be restless and constantly on the go almost as if I'm being driven by a motor engine, just like cars and big lorries.

I find it hard to sit still in my seat, particularly when I'm supposed to – at mealtimes, in lessons, restaurants and even cinemas.

I often feel a need to get up and walk, because I'm very easily bored. My parents sometimes struggle to find babysitters for me if they want to go out.

Just being with me can make you feel tired, as I always want to do something physical to help burn off all my energy.

Joining me in physical activities can also help you stay fit and healthy."

"Being 'hyper' means I can be very
boisterous and competitive on the
playground, which sometimes causes
me to fall out with friends."

"I am even more boisterous when I haven't had a good night's sleep.

It can be difficult to wind down after a day full of activity.

I really struggle to fall asleep, because I have thoughts racing through my mind like a motor engine. It's not just my body that's on the go – my mind is too.

I sometimes find myself counting again and again, wishing I could fall asleep. This makes me feel very tired in the mornings. I find it harder to focus and pay attention in class after very bad nights."

"Having ADHD means that I can
be noisy and like to talk a lot.

I am especially noisy at mealtimes and
even when I'm playing on my own.

Being noisy in the mornings wakes my
baby sisters, which annoys my mum."

"Not being shy of speaking can be a good thing. I am often the first person in my class to make a new pupil feel welcome.

Talking lots and having a big imagination is sometimes a good recipe for interesting conversations, especially with adults.

Sometimes, though, when speaking, I forget to take my time, hurrying to say all my thoughts and ideas before I forget them. This sometimes means my words sound very muddled.

When I speak in a loud voice or my words appear muddled, please do not be impatient with me. Just ask me to slow down.

If I'm really excited about my thoughts and ideas, sometimes I shout or speak in a loud voice. It is not because I have trouble hearing you – remind me to speak clearly and quietly."

"Having ADHD means I sometimes
rush through chores and schoolwork.
This can result in poor grades."

"Rushing through schoolwork means my handwriting can be difficult to read because it is very muddled.

When I have to do writing in class, I have a lot of ideas in my head but these sometimes get jumbled up in my brain and my work appears muddled on paper. Rushing through schoolwork to get to the next thing doesn't help much either."

"I find it very hard to wait my turn for things and quickly become impatient when asked to wait in a line."

"Grown-ups often call me 'fearless' or 'impulsive'. Being impulsive means I sometimes do or say things without thinking, which often gets me into trouble.

Waiting my turn in games is also a struggle and I soon lose interest if my turn doesn't come quickly enough or I'm losing a game.

I often interrupt conversations without meaning to. I don't mean to be rude. I sometimes forget to wait for someone to finish their sentence and feel silly afterwards when I can't give the right answer to a question, which means I wasn't listening in the first place."

"People with ADHD sometimes struggle to understand the consequences of their behaviour on others.

I sometimes behave in a silly way without thinking about the effect on others."

"Sometimes I do these things because I think they might make me more popular with my classmates.

Some of the 'daredevil' things I do are:

- Climbing trees and fences when I have been told countless times not to do so.

- Doing silly things as a dare when I am urged on by my classmates, particularly when we get temporary support teachers.

This means that I am known as the 'class clown' and it often gets me into trouble with the temporary teachers."

"I must always remember to check for traffic when crossing the road to avoid accidents."

"I need a lot of help at the roadside when cycling to school with my friends. Luckily, my home is not very far from school so I don't have to cross a busy road.

Roadside noises sometimes confuse me and I can get distracted when crossing a road. Roadside noises appear very loud in my ears. The school crossing patrol lady helps me to cross the road safely.

When cycling or walking by the roadside, I avoid things that can easily distract me – like talking on my phone, listening to music or even talking to my friends."

"Getting angry at things I don't need
to be angry about and then falling out
with my friends doesn't help either."

"When I'm angry I find it hard to control my feelings and I end up arguing with friends, family and even teachers. I sometimes get so upset that I cry really loudly and throw things about in anger.

I'm trying very hard to control my temper by counting quietly in my head. It is very important because I don't want to lose my friends or get into trouble, especially at football games. I hate it when I'm told to sit on the bench by my football coach.

I overheard the football coach telling my dad the other day that I sometimes behave younger than my age. That really upset me.

My anger outbursts mean some of the children in my class don't want to be around me. Sometimes I don't get invited to birthday parties.

At football games, sitting on the reserve bench helps me to cool down, even though I would rather be playing."

"Have you heard the term
'away with the fairies'?

This means that I often disappear into
my own make-believe or dream world."

"Having ADHD means that I have a very good imagination. I like to think and imagine all sorts of things I would rather be doing. This is why I'm sometimes called 'Benjie dreamer'.

My favourite places to 'dream' are at mealtimes and in the classroom, particularly when I find a lesson boring.

I sometimes take a long time to finish my breakfast, especially on school mornings.

At school, I struggle with subjects I find hard because I'm very easily distracted.

I find it especially hard to pay attention in class if there is a lot of noise in the classroom. I may find myself interrupting other people's conversations.

In order to focus, I sometimes make strange noises without thinking about it.

It is not a good idea if my desk is at the back of the class or near a window because then I can often spend a whole lesson looking out at what is going on outside and not paying attention."

"Having ADHD means I can be
forgetful and lose things very easily."

"In one school term I lost:

- two school bags

- four pencil cases

- three school blazers

- my reading glasses.

My parents were not very pleased, as they had to replace all these things.

When I'm asked to do a chore at home, I easily forget about what I'm supposed to be doing and do something completely different from what I was asked to do in the first place.

I sometimes get into trouble with my teachers for forgetting to bring my homework to school.

I now use a diary which has all the useful information about what I need for that day at school."

"A paediatrician is a special doctor who looks after children. He sees me regularly because I have ADHD."

"The paediatrician is very kind and listens very carefully to my parents and me. He looks at reports from school and even some from my football club.

When I visit the paediatrician, he asks me a lot of questions which aren't hard to answer. The paediatrician has given my parents and me a lot of information about ADHD.

A special teacher called an educational psychologist has assessed me and says that I have normal intelligence. The educational psychologist is pleased that I've been given a diagnosis of ADHD by my paediatrician.

The educational psychologist and the paediatrician have helped me and other people understand ADHD and, more importantly, how to support someone like me."

"The paediatrician told me that ADHD has
been around for years and years."

"A British doctor called George Still first described ADHD in 1902.

In 1845, a German doctor called Heinrich Hoffman wrote a poem about a very fidgety boy called 'Fidgety Philip'.

ADHD is more common in boys than girls.

There are no special blood tests or scans for ADHD.

People with ADHD have three main symptoms: attention problems, hyperactivity and impulsivity.

Some people may have all the main symptoms of ADHD; others may have two of the three main symptoms.

People with ADD (or ADHD without the 'H') often struggle more with being attentive. Girls more than boys tend to have this type of ADHD which makes it hard to spot.

To have ADHD, symptoms should occur in more than one place – for example, at school and at home. This is why a lot of reports are needed from different people to give an accurate picture of difficulties.

Having ADHD means that a child struggles to cope with everyday life in many different places. This can include school, at home and at clubs."

"What causes ADHD?

ADHD is not due to bad parenting
or eating certain foods.

It is, however, a very good idea to eat a
healthy diet and take regular exercise."

"ADHD runs in families and many children have a close family member with similar symptoms.

It is now known that ADHD is associated with changes in certain parts of the brain.

The brain is made up of tiny special cells that transfer chemical messages to different parts of the brain.

In ADHD, there is a problem with transferring these important chemical messages to parts of the brain that are important for attention and impulse control.

The paediatrician always involves me in discussions about ADHD. He gives my parents a lot of information to read about support in school and ADHD groups and he gives me books to read.

He offers advice on good diet and the importance of regular exercise in ADHD. It is good for the whole family to have a healthy lifestyle."

"Since receiving my ADHD diagnosis from the paediatrician I feel more confident.

I am happy that my parents, teachers and friends understand me more.

I'm a better team member in my football club as I listen to the coach more.

I get invited to more birthday parties and I have more friends.

Mum and Dad do not have any more problems with getting someone to babysit when they go out.

I concentrate better on my schoolwork and don't rush to finish it.

My reading, writing and schoolwork is improving and homework is not such a chore now.

Guess what? I won the gold award for the best-behaved boy in my class at the end of the school year.

This has made me the happiest boy in the whole wide world."

# More about ADHD

## ADHD AND OTHER CONDITIONS

"People with ADHD may also have other medical conditions such as genetic or thyroid disorders. They may also have low levels of iron due to a poor diet.

Sometimes blood tests and other tests may be necessary to determine these medical conditions.

It is very important to distinguish between ADHD and these other conditions as this can affect the help that can be given to someone with ADHD.

There are certain conditions that can mimic the symptoms of ADHD or co-exist with it. These conditions include learning difficulties such as dyslexia, sleep difficulties, coordination and motor problems (sometimes called dyspraxia), epilepsy, autism spectrum disorders, anxiety, depression, challenging behaviours and tic disorders.

Tics occur when there is sudden jerkiness or movement of a part or several parts of the body. These are called motor tics.

Vocal tics occur when a person repeatedly clears their throat or says something with very little control.

Excessive tics may be mistaken for ADHD. It is important to distinguish between ADHD and tics, as treating ADHD with certain types of medication may worsen tics."

## HOW MEDICATION CAN HELP

"It is now known that ADHD may be due to a chemical imbalance in the brain. Medication can help correct some of this chemical imbalance.

My ADHD medication helps to correct the chemical imbalance in my brain by increasing the amount of chemical messages to certain parts of my brain. These chemical messages are carried by special brain transmitters or messengers. The special messengers or brain transmitters are like postal workers (messengers) delivering special letters or parcels (chemical messages) to a home.

These messages are delivered to special parts of the brain responsible for attention, problem solving and impulse control.

Medication does not cure ADHD; it helps people with ADHD pay attention and focus more.

Medication also helps people with ADHD think more about the effect of their behaviour on other people.

Medication for ADHD is associated with some common side effects such as difficulty falling asleep, poor appetite, tummy aches and headaches.

Taking the medication may make me feel moody and sad.

It is important to talk to a doctor about any of these side effects.

Sometimes side effects are reduced when medication is taken with meals.

The paediatrician regularly monitors any side effects and changes he makes to my medication."

## SUPPORTING PEOPLE WITH ADHD

"It is important to note that ADHD management is not only about medication.

People with ADHD should receive support at home, school and clubs.

In less severe forms of ADHD, medication may not be needed at all. In severe ADHD where medication is needed, there is also need for support.

Support for a person with ADHD may include:

- Information for teachers on how to support children in the classroom, particularly if they're experiencing difficulties with learning.

- Referral of parents and carers to parent behaviour and support groups to learn how to help a person with ADHD.

- Children may be offered coaching on how to deal with their feelings, friends and listening to other people and on problem-solving techniques.

- Older teenagers may be offered a special form of counselling or therapy.

It is very important to include information that can be easily understood by a younger child with ADHD.

Information for the younger child should be presented in very simple language with lots of colourful pictures that can help them understand ADHD better."

# How friends can help

- "Remind me gently when I'm being noisy and bossy.

- Please let's avoid trouble altogether – it's not cool to be silly.

- Sometimes I may say things without thinking.

- Forgive me if I have not been listening.

- I will be happy if you invite me to your birthday party as I'm such fun to be with. I promise your party will be more fun with my charm and wit!

- Please don't tease me because I have ADHD.

- Getting help now means I'm getting better and better every day."

# How parents can help

## MANAGING BEHAVIOURS

- "Going to parent training and support groups and reading a lot of information about ADHD is a very good thing, because this will help you understand me better.

- Remember that some of my behaviours are not meant to be naughty – I sometimes cannot help myself. I am also aware that having ADHD is not an excuse for bad behaviour.

- Please remain calm when dealing with me. Being angry or shouting will make me more excited and defiant.

- Behaviour books and charts can help work out a list of achievable positive goals. Remember that targets may not only be about good behaviour. Simple things such as finishing homework, tidying up after play or meals and not interrupting conversations can all be achievable targets.

- It is also important that targets are achieved one at a time and not too many at once."

## REWARDS

- "Rewards and praise for good behaviour and complying with rules can help motivate me to do better. Please discuss any family rules and rewards with me in advance so things are clear to me.

- Rewards can be very simple things such as baking my favourite cake or inviting a friend over to play. It would also be nice if you involve me in identifying rewards."

## TIME OUT AND SANCTIONS

- "An area at home for 'time out' for stressful situations or unacceptable behaviour is better than being shouted at or told I'm being naughty. This can help calm me down, especially when I'm having outbursts.

- Sanctions can be used when 'time out' hasn't been successful in helping me calm down. Please remember to tell me why I'm receiving sanctions.

- Please avoid mentioning the behaviour once the sanction is over."

## KEEPING RULES AND INSTRUCTIONS CLEAR

- "It is very important for rules to be clear and consistent. Unclear rules confuse me and may cause misunderstanding between us.

- I need consistent routines as much as possible. Clear structures and limits should be communicated to any adult looking after me.

- Difficulties with attention may result in missing parts of instructions. It is important that instructions are clear, short and simple.

- Please maintain eye contact with me when giving instructions. Doing this will let you know I've heard and understood your instructions."

## HELPING ME TO BE MORE ORGANISED

- "Tick sheets with visual clues, planners, wall charts and Post-it notes in visible places may all be helpful reminders about regular chores, homework, taking medications and getting ready for school. They also help me organise myself better.

- Packing my schoolbag and laying out my school uniform the night before will help make school mornings smoother, reducing overall strain on my parents and me."

## DOING HOMEWORK

- "When doing homework, it is important that distractions such as television are minimised as I need to concentrate on my work. A special quiet area at home for homework is helpful.

- Please remember that children are able to concentrate on tasks for only a certain length of time.

- Short breaks from homework are good, as I find paying attention for long periods without a break very tiring."

## ROAD SAFETY

- "Children with ADHD can get very excited when outdoors. Roadside noises can be very overwhelming and distracting. It is very important to teach children with ADHD about roadside safety as soon as they are old enough to understand."

## FAMILY BONDING AND BEDTIME ROUTINES

- "There are a lot of family games involving memory and concentration which can help improve my attention levels. Family games are also good for family bonding.

- Games involving taking turns will teach me the importance of waiting for my turn, especially when I am with my friends.

- A regular bedtime routine will help me relax. It is very important to avoid stimulating drinks such as tea, coffee or other drinks containing caffeine at bedtime. Instead, a soothing drink, such as warm milk, may help me fall asleep more quickly.

- Lights in the bedroom need to be completely off or very low.

- Sounds should be kept to a minimum."

## GETTING ACTIVE AND FIT

- "As I have lots of energy, very physical activities such as swimming, tennis, trampolining and even martial arts can help release my pent-up energy.

- Martial arts can help with concentration and discipline with controlling anger outbursts.

- Physical activities can also improve coordination and motor problems that occur with ADHD."

## INCLUDE SIBLINGS, FAMILY MEMBERS AND SCHOOL

- "Remember to include siblings, family and close family friends in understanding ADHD and how they can help me.

- Please remember to tell school that I have ADHD and I am on medication for it, so they can help monitor my progress."

## CELEBRATE MY STRENGTHS AND ACHIEVEMENTS

- "Continue to help me celebrate my strengths and achievements.

- This will help me remember that despite having ADHD I am good at a lot of things. My achievements will make me feel more confident and motivate me to do better and better."

# How teachers can help

## GOOD COMMUNICATION

- "It is very important for school and my parents to communicate regularly about my progress. Knowing how my day has been can help prevent future conflicts with friends, adults and siblings.

- I may not pay attention in class because of poor sleep the night before. It would be helpful sometimes for teachers to ask my mum or dad whether I've had a good night's sleep. Understanding the way I'm feeling following a poor night may also help prevent arguments with friends during playtime."

## MINIMISING DISTRACTIONS

"Like many children with ADHD, I can be easily distracted.

- In the classroom, place me away from distractions – for example, windows or other pupils who are easily distracted.

- People with ADHD commonly demonstrate poor working memory. This means that we find it difficult to process and retain certain types of information. Instructions given by teachers should be short, clear and concise. It may be a good idea to ask me to repeat back instructions, checking that I've heard and understood them.

- Please ensure you sustain eye contact with me when giving me instructions."

## BREAKING DOWN TASKS

- "Tasks should be broken down into small chunks in class. This will help me take my time when writing and recording my ideas on paper.

- Praise and rewards given immediately will help boost my confidence and self-esteem."

## IN THE CLASSROOM

- "Transition times and lesson changes can be highly distracting for people with ADHD. Support during changes in lessons will keep me on task and help me avoid getting into trouble.

- Check lists and planners will help me become more organised with my schoolwork.

- A fellow pupil who is not easily distracted can be chosen as a role model to help support me.

- Class activities that require large groups may be very distracting for me. In such situations, paired groupings may be a much better idea to help minimise distractions.

- It may be necessary sometimes to allow additional time for completing projects and assignments. Extra time may also be needed in examinations.

- Allowing me to fiddle with my 'stress ball' in class and stressful situations can help calm me down. Fiddling with my special ball can help me stay focused on teachers during lessons.

- It is important for teachers to make lessons interesting and stimulating to help maintain attention and focus in people with ADHD.

- I should be encouraged to ask for help more easily, especially when I don't understand a task."

## PLAYTIME

- "Waiting my turn during games can be hard sometimes. Please be patient and remind me that it is important that we take turns, so that everyone can enjoy the game. Reminding me that other people also need to wait like me is also helpful."

# Recommended reading, organisations and websites

## BOOKS

Green, Christopher and Chee, Kit (1997) *Understanding ADHD: A Parent's Guide to Attention Deficit Hyperactivity Disorder in Children*. London: Vermillion.

Hoopman, Kathy (2009) *All Dogs Have ADHD*. London: Jessica Kingsley Publishers.

Kewley, Geoff D. (1999) *Attention Deficit Hyperactivity Disorder: Recognition, Reality and Resolution*. London: David Fulton Publishers.

Nadeau, Kathleen G. and Dixon, Ellen B. (2002) *Learning to Slow Down and Pay Attention: A Book for Kids about ADHD*. Washington, DC: Magination Press.

Quinn, Patricia and Stern, Judith (1991) *Putting on the Brakes: Young People's Guide to Understanding Attention Deficit Hyperactivity Disorder (ADHD)*. Washington, DC: Magination Press.

Quinn, Patricia and Stern, Judith (2009) *Putting on the Brakes: Understanding and Taking Control of Your ADD/ADHD*. Washington, DC: Magination Press.

Weaver, Chris (1998) *Full of Beans.* Concord West, Australia: Shrink-Rap Press.

Yarney, Susan (2012) *Rainbow: A Fictional Book about ADD/ADHD in Girls.* Published independently with an educational grant. For more details, contact the author at: susan.yarney@yahoo.co.uk.

Yarney, Susan (2012) *The Special Brain: A Fictional Book for Children about Understanding ADHD Neurobiology.* Published independently with an educational grant. For more details, contact the author at: susan.yarney@yahoo.co.uk.

Yemula, C.R. (2007) *Everything a Child Needs to Know about ADHD (Second edition).* Edgware: ADDISS UK.

## ORGANISATIONS AND WEBSITES

### UK

**ADDISS**
The National Attention Deficit Disorder Information and Support Service
Premier House
112 Station Road
Edgware
Middlesex
HA8 7BJ
Telephone: 020 8952 2800
Website: www.addiss.co.uk

**Family Lives**
Telephone: 0808 800 2222.
Website: http://familylives.org.uk

**Living with ADHD**
Living with ADHD
Janssen-Cilag Ltd
50-100 Holmers Farm Way
High Wycombe
Buckinghamshire
HP12 4EG
Website: www.livingwithadhd.co.uk

# USA
### Chadd (Children and Adults with Attention-Deficit/ Hyperactivity Disorder)
CHAD National Office
8181 Professional Place - Suite 150
Landover
MD 20785
Telpehone: 800-233-4050
Website:  www.chadd.org

**ADDvance**
Website: www.addvance.com

## International
### ADD/ADHD Online Information
Website: www.adders.org

Blank, for your notes

Blank, for your drawings